DISCARD

WILDERNESS
SURVIVAL SKILLS

GETTING RESCUED
IN THE WILD

WILLIAM DECKER

PowerKiDS
press.

New York

Published in 2016 by The Rosen Publishing Group, Inc.
29 East 21st Street, New York, NY 10010

First Edition

Editor: Sarah Machajewski
Book Design: Michael J. Flynn

Photo Credits: Cover Dudarev Mikhail/Shutterstock.com; cover, pp. 1, 3–4, 6, 8, 10, 12, 14, 16, 18–20, 22–24 (map background) Sergei Drozd/Shutterstock.com; p. 4 Gary S Chapman/Photodisc/Getty Images; p. 5 gorillaimages/Shutterstock.com; p. 7 Wessel du Plooy/Shutterstock.com; p. 8 Martin Novak/Shutterstock.com; p. 9 (tool background) Falcon Eyes/Shutterstock.com; p. 9 (notepad) Evgeny Karandaev/Shutterstock.com; p. 10 Aleksandra Gigowska/Shutterstock.com; p. 11 andreiuc88/Shutterstock.com; p. 12 Peter Mason/Shutterstock.com; p. 13 Cultura RM/Seth K. Hughes/Cultura/Getty Images; p. 14 svand/Shutterstock.com; p. 15 © iStockphoto.com/shaunl; p. 16 Anton Gvozdikov/Shutterstock.com; p. 17 Nejron Photo/Shutterstock.com; p. 18 Verity E. Milligan/Moment Open/Getty Images; p. 19 Perfect Lazybones/Shutterstock.com; p. 20 https://commons.wikimedia.org/wiki/File:Signal_Mirror_Glass_USAF_MIL-M-18371E_Type_II.JPEG; p. 21 Simon Bottomley/Digital Vision/Getty Images; p. 22 Mikadun/Shutterstock.com.

Cataloging-in-Publication Data

Decker, William.
Getting rescued in the wild / by William Decker.
p. cm. — (Wilderness survival skills)
Includes index.
ISBN 978-1-5081-4315-4 (pbk.)
ISBN 978-1-5081-4317-8 (6-pack)
ISBN 978-1-5081-4318-5 (library binding)
1. Wilderness survival — Juvenile literature. 2. Rescue work — Juvenile literature. I. Decker, William (William Anthony), 1983-. II. Title.
GV200.5 D44 2016
613.6'9—d23

Manufactured in the United States of America

CPSIA Compliance Information: Batch #BW16PK: For Further Information contact Rosen Publishing, New York, New York at 1-800-237-9932

CONTENTS

A NOTE TO READERS

Always talk with a parent or teacher before proceeding with any of the activities found in this book. Some activities require adult supervision.

A NOTE TO PARENTS AND TEACHERS

This book was written to be informative and entertaining. Some of the activities in this book require adult supervision. Please talk with your child or student before allowing them to proceed with any wilderness activities. The authors and publisher specifically disclaim any liability for injury or damages that may result from use of information in this book.

EXPLORING THE NATURAL WORLD

What comes to mind when you think of the **wilderness**? You may picture camping in a forest or hiking on a mountain. You may picture an open beach, **stretches** of desert, or a snowy **environment**. Our planet has many places to explore—where do you want to go?

Exploring nature is a fun way to spend your time. However, there are **risks** that come along with entering the wilderness, no matter what environment it is. This book will cover survival skills that will keep you safe while you're exploring.

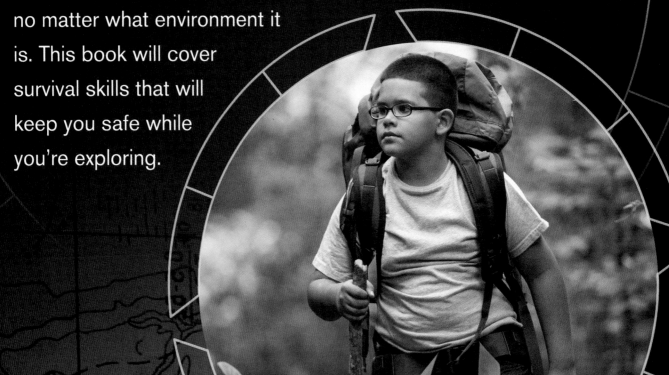

There are many ways to enjoy the "great outdoors," which is a term some people use to talk about the wilderness.

SURVIVING ANYTHING

A survival skill is anything that helps you stay alive in a dangerous, or unsafe, **situation**. Survival skills include finding water and food, building **shelter**, making tools, knowing first aid, and more.

One important survival skill is knowing how to get rescued, or saved, from the wilderness if you need to. There's no way to know what you'll face when you enter the wilderness—you may get hurt, sick, or lost. Knowing what to do in these situations will help you survive them.

SURVIVAL TIP

Practice some survival skills, such as learning how to read a map, before going into the wilderness. That way, your skills will be ready to use when you need them.

Being aware of your surroundings and the conditions of the environment you're in are two important ways to stay safe outdoors.

PACKING AND PREPARING

Before you head out into the wilderness, spend time preparing. Being prepared means you're ready to face any situation that may happen. This includes bringing water, food, and all your gear.

When you're preparing, think about what would help you in a rescue situation. A rescue whistle can be very helpful. Fire-starting tools are great to have on hand. Flashlights, mirrors, and brightly colored objects can help, too. These are just a few examples of things to bring with you in the wilderness.

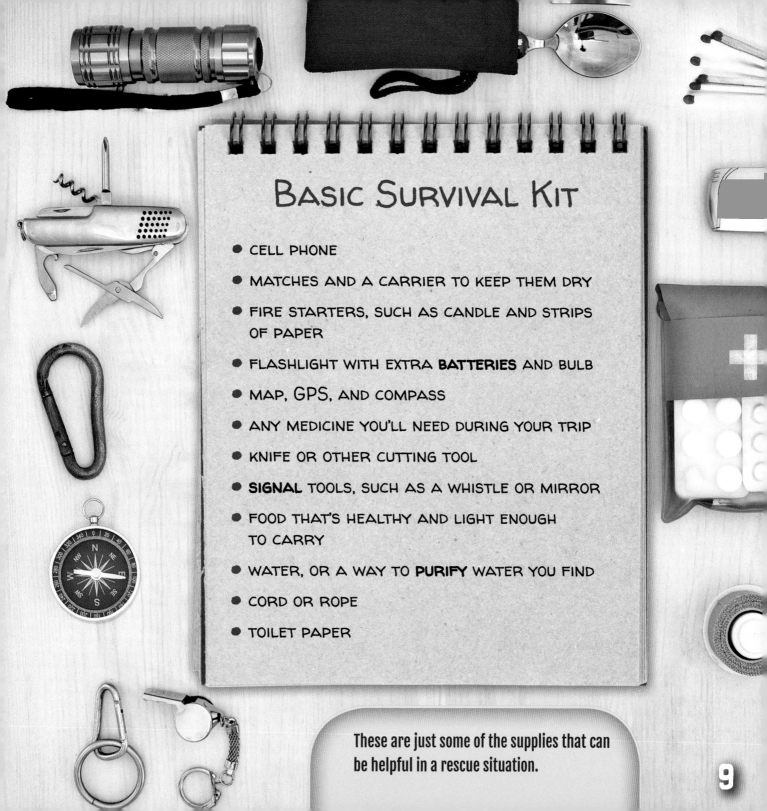

Basic Survival Kit

- CELL PHONE
- MATCHES AND A CARRIER TO KEEP THEM DRY
- FIRE STARTERS, SUCH AS CANDLE AND STRIPS OF PAPER
- FLASHLIGHT WITH EXTRA **BATTERIES** AND BULB
- MAP, GPS, AND COMPASS
- ANY MEDICINE YOU'LL NEED DURING YOUR TRIP
- KNIFE OR OTHER CUTTING TOOL
- **SIGNAL** TOOLS, SUCH AS A WHISTLE OR MIRROR
- FOOD THAT'S HEALTHY AND LIGHT ENOUGH TO CARRY
- WATER, OR A WAY TO **PURIFY** WATER YOU FIND
- CORD OR ROPE
- TOILET PAPER

These are just some of the supplies that can be helpful in a rescue situation.

FIRST THINGS FIRST

Despite your planning, it isn't hard to get lost or hurt when you're in the wilderness. Many people think it will never happen to them, but it does.

If you're hurt or think you're lost, the most important thing is to stay calm. This will allow you to think through your next steps. Panicking won't help you think clearly. New York State forest rangers tell people to think of the word "STOP." It's an easy way to remember what to do next.

EMERGENCY CALL

911

SURVIVAL TIP

If you have a cell phone, dial 911. Sometimes emergency services can pick up a call even when you don't think it will go through.

STOP!

S SIT DOWN

This helps your body and mind calm down. Panicking will only make your situation worse.

T THINK

Play back the day in your mind. How did you get to where you are? Have you been in this place before?

O OBSERVE

Look for any natural features, such as mountains, that can give you a sense of where you are. Listen for people, traffic, or running water. Do you notice anything that will help you get back to safety?

P PLAN

Should you try to get out of the wilderness, or should you stay put until the next day? How much time do you have until it gets dark?

Each letter in the word "STOP" stands for something that will help you when you're lost or hurt. This will help you stay calm in a scary situation.

STAYING ALIVE

Let's say you can't leave the wilderness safely. You have to stay put—either because you don't know where you are or because it's getting dark soon. What's the first thing you should do? Gather firewood—you'll need to make a fire, and it's easier to gather wood while it's still light out.

Next, build shelter. It will keep you safe from bad weather and more. Your goal now is to stay alive until you're rescued.

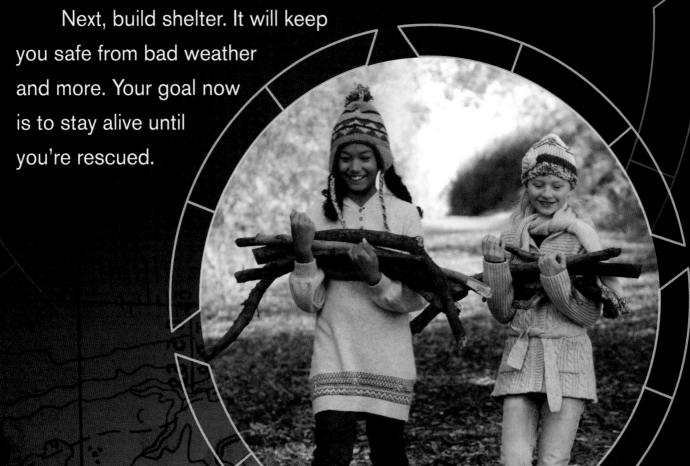

Make sure to drink plenty of water. Dehydration, or when your body doesn't have enough water, can kill you. Make sure to eat something, too. You need to keep your **energy** up.

BUILDING FIRE

Fire is one of the most important tools in a rescue situation. Light is easily seen at night, and smoke is easily seen during the day. Build three fires in a triangle. This is an international distress signal, which means no matter where you are, people who see this will know you need help.

Build your fires in a clear area where they can be easily seen. You can use the fires' smoke as a signal, too. Burning plant matter creates white smoke, while burning rubber or oil creates black smoke.

Signal fires are much different from a campfire. They're bigger, taller, and are more easily spotted from faraway locations.

Three **columns** of smoke are another international distress signal. In fact, any object set up in threes can be taken as a sign that someone needs help.

USING THE LAND

You've built shelter and fire, and you've rested. Now it's time to focus on getting rescued. Look for the highest point in your environment, such as a mountain or hill. Get as high as you can, and look around. Do you see any signs of **civilization**? If so, you know where you need to go.

You can also listen for water. Follow a river or stream, which will likely flow into a bigger body of water. People live and gather around water, so it will likely bring you to a civilized area.

Use the wilderness's natural features, such as flowing water or high mountains or hills, to help you. They'll guide your path to being rescued.

SURVIVAL TIP

It may be easier for rescuers to see you if you're somewhere high rather than among tall trees or plants that make it hard to see you.

SIGNS OF LIFE

If you're lost in the wilderness, people are going to be looking for you. If you want to be found, you must leave signs that you're there. Rescuers will look for signs of life, such as footprints, smoke, and more.

Think about what will help rescuers find you. Fly a brightly colored flag or piece of clothing, or spread them out in a place where they can be seen. If you can find it, burn matter that will create black smoke.

If you're in an open area, spell the word "HELP" large enough for rescuers to see. Use sticks, rocks, clothes, or anything you can find in your environment to create this giant message.

SURVIVAL TIP

Use colors that stand out from the rest of your environment. For example, a red shirt on yellow sand will stand out. Black smoke during the daytime will stand out against a light background.

19

OTHER WAYS TO SIGNAL

If you've packed the right tools, they can help you get rescued. Making lots of noise is one way to help rescuers find you. Use a rescue whistle—it's been said they can be heard up to 1 mile (1.6 km) away. Flares and flashlights are good tools, too.

Use a mirror or other shiny object to signal. Hold the object up to the sun. Catch the light, which will bounce off the object in the other direction. Wiggle the object so the light flashes. Someone searching overhead should easily see this.

Carry your mirror or other shiny object on a string around your neck. If you're hurt or unable to walk, you have an important rescue tool right at your side.

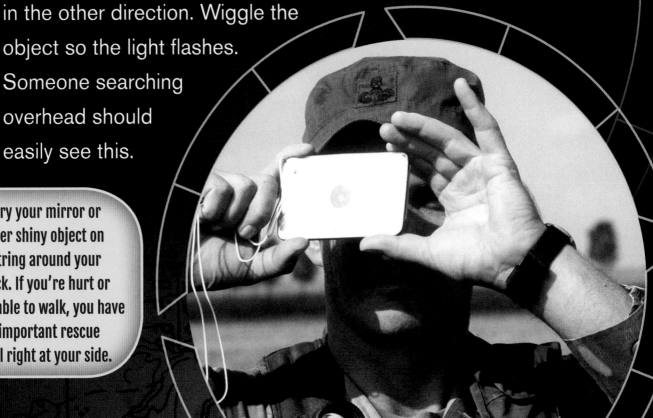

SURVIVAL TIP

A flare is a tool that creates a bright burst of light. Bring one with you the next time you go into the wilderness.

IMPROVING YOUR CHANCES

You can make your chances of getting rescued much better if you follow this important tip: *always tell someone what your plans are.* Tell them where you're going and when you plan on returning. This will give people a starting point when they begin searching for you.

If you're in a survival situation, the key to getting rescued is to **attract** attention. Getting lost or hurt in the wilderness can be really scary. If you stay calm, you can come up with a plan to get rescued.

GLOSSARY

attract: To draw.

battery: A source of power.

civilization: Society; people.

column: A tall, upright object.

energy: The power to do work.

environment: The surroundings in which a person, animal, or plant lives.

purify: To make clean.

risk: Something that could put someone in an unsafe situation.

shelter: A place that keeps a person safe from bad weather.

signal: An action or sound used to show someone something. Also, to show someone something using an action or sound.

situation: A series of events in which a person finds himself or herself.

stretch: A continuous area of land or water.

wilderness: A natural, wild place.

INDEX

A
attract attention, 22

C
cell phone, 9, 10
civilization, 16

D
distress signal, 14, 15

F
fire, 12, 14, 16
fire-starting tools, 8, 9
flares, 20, 21
flashlight, 8, 9, 20
food, 6, 8, 9
forest, 4, 10

H
hurt, 6, 10, 11, 20, 22

L
lost, 6, 10, 11, 18, 22

M
mirrors, 8, 9, 20
mountain, 4, 11, 16

R
rescue whistle, 8, 9, 20

S
shelter, 6, 12, 16
signs of life, 18
smoke, 14, 15, 18, 19
STOP, 10, 11

T
tell someone, 22
threes, 14, 15

W
water, 6, 8, 9, 11, 13, 16

WEBSITES